The Little Queen

Stewart Ross
Illustrated by Sue Shields

WAYLAND

Little Princess Vicky was fast asleep.

Titles in this series
Hal the Hero
The Little Queen

First published in 1999 by
Wayland Publishers Ltd
61 Western Road, Hove
East Sussex BN3 1JD, England

This edition published in 2000

Series editor: Alex Woolf
Book designer: Jean Wheeler

British Library Cataloguing in Publication Data
Ross, Stewart
  The little Queen : the amazing story of Queen Victoria.
  (Stories from history)
  1.Victoria, Queen of Great Britain - Juvenile literature
  2.Queens - Great Britain - Biography - Juvenile literature
  3.Great Britain - History - Victoria, 1837-1901 - Juvenile
  literature
  941'.081'092

ISBN 0 7502 2647 1

Typeset by Jean Wheeler
Printed and bound in Portugal by Edições ASA

Her mother woke her up.

A man had news for Vicky.

Vicky was now the Little Queen!

The Little Queen put on a big crown.

She was very grown up.

The Little Queen was bored. She wanted a friend.

One day she met Prince Bertie.

and got married.

Vicky and Bertie were very happy.

Vicky and Bertie had nine children.

Prince Bertie did many useful things.

But one day Bertie fell ill.

Prince Bertie died. Vicky was very, very sad.

The Little Queen did not smile.
She did not see anyone.

The people were angry with the Little Queen.

They said she was a bad queen.

Then a kind man made Vicky smile.

She was happy again!

The Little Queen waved to the crowds,

Hello people!

and the crowds waved back.

There was a big party in London.

People came from all over the world.

Queen Vicky loved them all,

Do you know?

This story is TRUE!
The queen was called VICTORIA. Her husband was called ALBERT.
Victoria was Queen of Great Britain 100 years ago.
This is what she looked like when she was a young woman:

Notes for adults

The Little Queen and the National Curriculum.

The Little Queen grew out of the ideas presented in two recent documents: the Department for Education and Employment's *National Literacy Strategy* and the Qualifications and Curriculum Authority's *Maintaining Breadth and Balance at Key Stages 1 and 2*. It is both a Key Stage 1 reader, offering stimulating material for use during the Literacy Hour, and a useful springboard for Key Stage 1 history. In presenting the story of Queen Victoria in the simplest possible terms, it introduces the child to one of the best-known figures from British history, and presents many opportunities for (a) 'looking for similarities and differences between life today and – in the past', (b) 'talking and writing about what happened and why people acted as they did', and (c) 'finding out about the past using different sources of information and representations'. (*Maintaining Breadth and Balance*, p. 10.)

Suggested follow-up activities

1. Checking the child knows and can use words they might not have come across before. In particular:

prince	hooray	sweetie	goodbye
asleep	princess	snore	everyone
crown	idea	angry	bored
anyone	hello	people	smile
wise	crowd	useful	listen

2. Talking about things remaining from Victoria's time, e.g. buildings (schools, churches, offices, railway stations), the *Great Britain*, the Albert Hall, furniture, the portrait of Victoria (opposite), etc.

3. Discussing how we know about Victoria, i.e. sources (perhaps starting with the portrait).

4. Explaining the exact dates of Victoria's reign (1837–1901) and what they mean.

5. Going further into aspects of Victoria's reign, e.g. Jubilees, the British Empire and Victoria's title Empress of India, technological developments (railways, steam ships, etc.), and the spread of education and nature of Victorian schooling.

6. Comparing life in Victorian Britain with today, e.g. clothing, school life, sailing ships, steam engines, gas lights.